AFTER HOUR

FOR SOLO PIANO

BOOK 3

PAM WEDGWOOD

© 2003 by Faber Music Ltd
First published in 2003 by Faber Music Ltd
3 Queen Square London WC1N 3AU
Cover by Velladesign
Piano provided courtesy of J Reid Pianos
Printed in England by Caligraving Ltd
All rights reserved

ISBN 0-571-52259-9

To buy Faber Music publications or to find out about the full range of titles available
please contact your local music retailer or Faber Music sales enquiries:

Faber Music Limited, Burnt Mill, Elizabeth Way, Harlow, CM20 2HX England
Tel: +44 (0)1279 82 89 82   Fax: +44 (0)1279 82 89 83
sales@fabermusic.com   fabermusic.com

CONTENTS

FORGOTTEN DREAMS

With feeling ♩ = 72

Pam Wedgwood

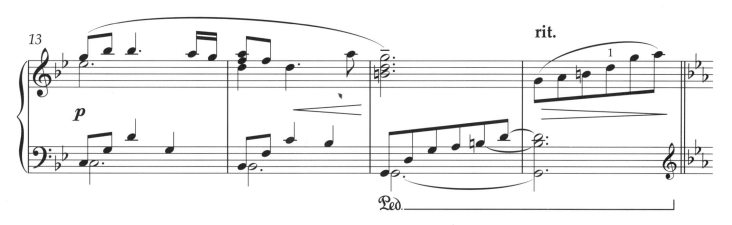

WILD POPPIES

FLINDERS STREET

FALLING

SLIDING DOORS

With a strong rhythmic feel ♩ = 132

HANG-UP

STRANGE ENCOUNTER

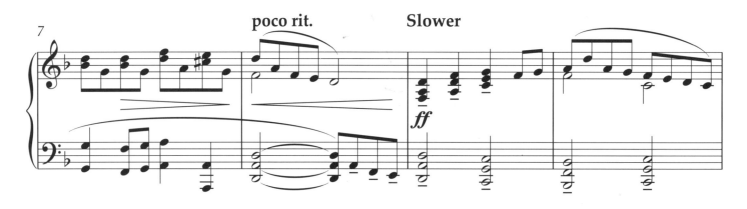

THE FRIENDS

Peacefully ♩. = 62

MESSAGE IN A BOTTLE

WATERFALLS

With movement ♩ = 78

poco rit. a tempo

SLEEP LITTLE BABY

TABLE FOR 2

Relaxed, with feeling ♩ = 76

CUNNING MR FOX

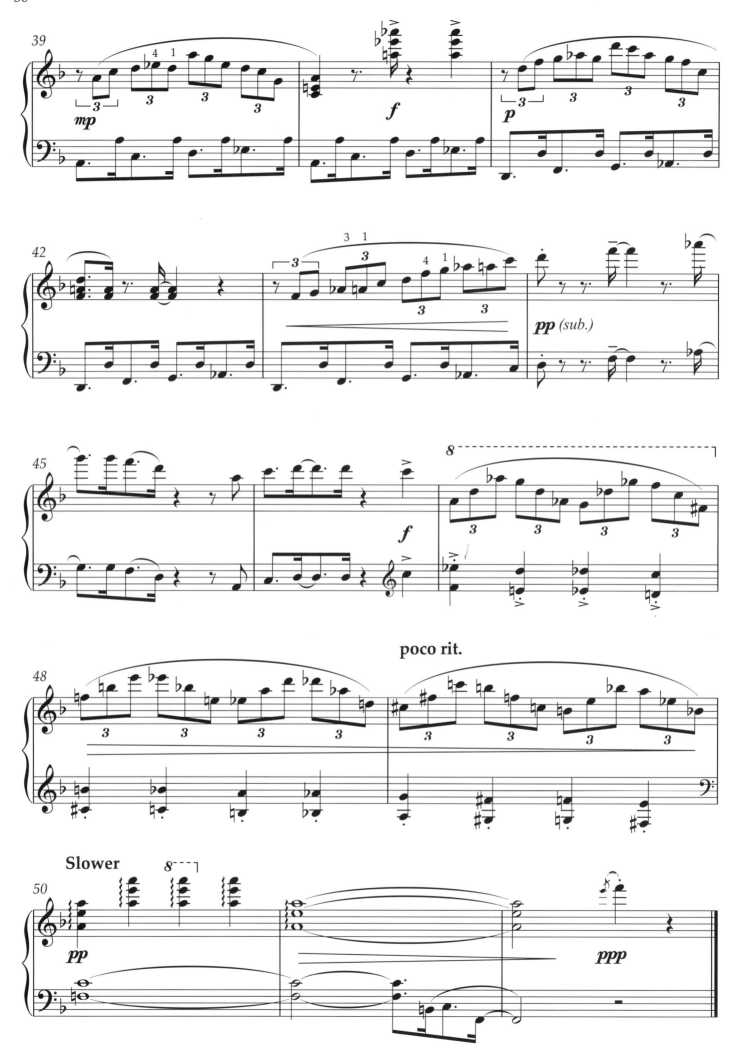

AFTER HOURS

In the darkness of the night ♩ = 66